# Bygone Bar Harbor

## A Postcard Tour of

Blairmyre, Bar Harbor, Me. Residence of D.

# MOUNT DESERT ISLAND & ACADIA NATIONAL PARK

## • BY EARL BRECHLIN •

DOWN EAST BOOKS • CAMDEN, MAINE

To brother Carl
who sparked my interest in
all things old and cool.

LIBRARY OF CONGRESS CONTROL NUMBER: 2001098372

ISBN 0-89272-543-5

COVER AND BOOK DESIGN BY LURELLE CHEVERIE

PRINTED IN CHINA

RPS

2   4   6   8   9   7   5   3

DOWN EAST BOOKS
P.O. BOX 679, CAMDEN ME 04849

BOOK ORDERS: 1-800-685-7962
WWW.DOWNEASTBOOKS.COM

**Preface** More than a century ago, long before people began lugging around early Kodak Brownie cameras, postcards were a favorite way to document trips and adventures. People collected as well as sent postcards to be able to share with others the wonders and sights they had seen. The bright colors—some postcards were even tinted by hand—allowed people to relive their trip and bring their friends and families along, over and over.

The popularity of postcards exploded, with numerous merchants and photographers competing to offer the widest selection and most unique views. Initially, many of the cards were produced in Germany. Later, printers in the United States got in on the craze. Most of the cards in this book come from the peak postcard period, between 1905 and 1920.

Because of its popularity as a watering hole for the rich and famous, Bar Harbor in its Golden Age was one of the most photographed locations in Maine. Everything—from the steamships to the hotels to the natural wonders of an island that would later become home to Acadia National Park—

was photographed and turned into a postal card, which could be mailed for a penny. Today, these postcards are recognized not just for their historical content but also as works of art in and of themselves.

For the people of today, collecting antique postcards from Bar Harbor—or from anywhere, for that matter—is a comparatively inexpensive way to hold onto a piece of the past. The affection engendered by postcards creates a bond to the past in much the same way that the beauty and history of these special places continue to hold onto our hearts. The images in this book, although not intended to be a comprehensive scholarly collection, do provide a wonderful taste, a visual sampling if you will, of the way things were in Bar Harbor and on Mount Desert Island almost a hundred years ago. In that respect they allow people of today to take a trip not only to a place they love and know well, or may one day hope to visit, but also back to another time.

All postcards are from the author's collection unless otherwise noted.

DOWNTOWN

# Bar Harbor

NUMBERS CORRESPOND
TO POSTCARDS

Bar Harbor
(Frenchman Bay)

The Bar

Eddy Brook

TOWN PIER

BRIDGE ST.

WEST ST.

COTTAGE ST.

MAIN ST.

THE FIELD

SHORE PATH

STEPHENS LN.

RODICK PLACE

ALBERT MEADOW

KENNEBEC ST.

HIGH ST.

ROBERT'S AVE.

DERBY LANE

ATLANTIC AVE.

HOLLAND AVE.

MT. DESERT ST.

LEDGELAWN AVE.

GLEN MARY RD.

AMORY LN.

EDEN ST.

EAGLE LAKE RD.

KEBO ST.

SPRING ST.

PLEASANT ST.

2nd SOUTH ST.

EDGEWOOD ST.

HANCOCK ST.

WAYMAN LANE

LIVINGSTON RD.

BARBERRY LN.

PARK ST.

N

0        1/8

MILE
(APPROXIMATE)

PRIVATE PROPERTIES
NOT INCLUDED ON MAP.

CROMWELL HBR. RD.

Cromwell Cove

1. BAR HARBOR, WHICH UNTIL 1918 WAS OFFICIALLY NAMED EDEN, IS SEEN FROM STRAWBERRY HILL LOOKING NORTH OVER THE ATHLETIC FIELDS TOWARD BAR ISLAND. EDEN WAS FOUNDED ON APRIL 4, 1796, WHEN THE NORTHERN HALF OF THE ISLAND SPLIT OFF FROM THE TOWN OF MOUNT DESERT.

Bar Harbor, Maine.   Birdseye View from Strawberry Hill.

2. U.S. NAVY TORPEDO BOATS AND DESTROYERS LIE AT ANCHOR IN FRENCHMAN BAY OFF BAR HARBOR, WHERE THE U.S. NAVY'S GREAT WHITE FLEET WAS A FREQUENT VISITOR. TODAY, MORE THAN FOUR DOZEN OCEAN LINERS, EACH CARRYING MORE THAN 1,000 PASSENGERS, CALL EVERY YEAR.

Harbor View showing U. S. War Vessels.

*Greetings from Bar Harbor, Me.*

Published by Chisholm Bros., Portland, Me. No 300.

3. The arrival of a Maine Central Railroad steamer from the rail terminus at Hancock Point, across the bay, was always a big event. The names of those disembarking on the wharf, today's town pier, were published regularly in the local paper.

Arrival of Boat at Bar Harbor, Me.
216166

4. Private wharves and piers clogged Bar Harbor, as shown in this view looking west from the site of the present-day town pier. Passenger steamers, private yachts, and even canoes were everywhere. Today, excursion and whale-watching boats share dock space with private yachts, lobster boats, and kayaks.

Bar Harbor, M.E.
Docks at Bar Harbor.

5. This view of the Maine Central Railroad wharf, taken from the foot of what is now Agamont Park, shows an early souvenir stand at the terminal facilities. Today, commercial sales are banned on the town pier, which now occupies the spot.

M. C. R. R. Wharf, Bar Harbor, Me.

16627

6. Getting onto Mount Desert Island by road was not for the faint of heart near the turn of the twentieth century. This toll bridge was finally taken over by Hancock County in 1917. Today's modern bridge is the third to span the narrows from Trenton to Thompson Island.

Mt. Desert Bridge, Maine. One of the few toll bridges now in existence

7. Nestled beneath Dry Mountain (center) and Green Mountain (right; today's Dorr and Cadillac), the village of Bar Harbor is framed by trees on Rodick Island. Once the site of numerous homes, fields, and fish houses, the island (now known as Bar Island) is owned by Acadia National Park, with the exception of one private residence.

Bar Harbor, Me.

8. Bar Harbor's swank swimming club, with its shoreside saltwater pool, is viewed from across the gravel bar (exposed at low tide) that connects Bar Island to Bar Harbor. The large hotel in the center is the St. Sauveur, on Mount Desert Street. The hotel was built in 1870 and torn down in 1945. The road at the far right is Bridge Street. Courtesy of the Bar Harbor Historical Society.

The Swimming Tank and St. Sauveur Hotel, Bar Harbor, Me.

9. Fish weirs used to catch herring were once a common sight along the Maine coast. Exposed twice a day by twelve-foot tides, the gravel bar between the town and Rodick Island, now Bar Island, was an easy place to build and maintain weirs.

Bar Harbor, Maine.  The Bar and Town from Rodicks Island.

10. THREE OF THE TOWN'S STATELY SUMMER HOMES GRACED THE SHORE WHERE BRIDGE STREET MEETS THE BAR. DESPITE THE LARGE SIZE OF THESE STRUCTURES, SOME BOASTING MORE THAN TWO DOZEN ROOMS, SERVANTS' QUARTERS, AND ELABORATE GROUNDS, THEY WERE REFERRED TO AS "COTTAGES."

Bar Harbor Bar, Bar Harbor, Me.

11. Bar Harbor's Village Green, on the left, still sports the E. Howard and Company clock donated by the Village Improvement Society. The view is looking north down Main Street from the corner of Mount Desert Street. The Grand Central Hotel occupied the block prior to it being given over to public space. The wooden hotel, built in 1873, was torn down in 1906.

BAR HARBOR, Me. Main Street from Village Green.

12. BAR HARBOR'S FIRE STATION ON FIREFLY LANE, NEAR THE VILLAGE GREEN, WAS DESIGNED BY ARCHITECT FRED SAVAGE. BUILT IN 1912, IT WAS HOME TO STEAM-POWERED FIRE ENGINES AND TEAMS OF HORSES. THE TOP OF THE TOWER WAS REMOVED IN 1951. TODAY, THE BUILDING SPORTS AN ADDITION ON THE EAST (RIGHT) SIDE THAT HOUSES THE POLICE DEPARTMENT AND PUBLIC REST ROOMS. COURTESY OF THE BAR HARBOR HISTORICAL SOCIETY.

Engine House, Bar Harbor, Me.

13. MAIN STREET WAS A BUSY PLACE IN THE EARLY PART OF THE TWENTIETH CENTURY. CENSUS RECORDS SHOW THAT MORE PEOPLE LIVED IN BAR HARBOR IN 1900 THAN IN 1990. THE ORIGINAL FIRST NATIONAL BANK BUILDING, WITH ITS WHITE COLUMNS (CENTER), WAS HAILED AS THE TOWN'S FIRST "FIRE-PROOF" STRUCTURE. TWO BUILDINGS DOWN TO THE LEFT HOUSE THE CURRENT BAR HARBOR BANKING AND TRUST COMPANY.

Main Street, Bar Harbor, Maine.

14. Traffic was heavy on Mount Desert Street in front of the Bar Harbor Congregational Church just five years after a bitter political fight that ended with automobiles being allowed onto Mount Desert Island. The church, built in 1888, burned in 1942.

COURTESY OF THE BAR HARBOR HISTORICAL SOCIETY.

'24

CONGREGATIONAL CHURCH, MT. DESERT ST., BAR HARBOR, ME.

15. The Casino, at the corner of Bridge and Cottage Streets, was a focal point of the community. Built in 1901, it was used for town meetings, social events, and the Way Bak Ball. It was torn down in 1970. The site is a parking lot today.

Bar Harbor, Maine. The Casino and Bridge Street.

16. Bar Harbor's spectacular wooden Building
of the Arts, designed by Guy Lowell, was built in
1907 at the south end of Hamilton Hill, adjacent
to the Kebo Valley Golf Course. The building,
which was used for music and drama performances,
burned in the Great Fire of 1947. A flat, open site,
now private property, is all that remains.

Art Building, Bar Harbor, Me.

17. Canoes upside down on a float on the harbor hint of one of the favorite pastimes at the turn of the twentieth century. In 1900 the Canoe Club boasted more than 300 members. Paddling lessons were taught by area Native Americans. Homes on Rodick Island, now Bar Island, can be seen in the background.

Bar Island, Bar Harbor, Me.

16613

18. THE TOWN BEACH AND BEGINNINGS OF THE SHORE PATH, IN THE FOREGROUND, LOOK MUCH THE SAME TODAY. WHAT HAS CHANGED ARE THE BUILDINGS. THE NEWPORT HOUSE (LEFT), WHICH WAS BUILT IN 1869, WAS TORN DOWN IN 1938. THERE IS A PARKING LOT AT THE SITE TODAY. THE TALL TOWER (RIGHT) WAS ON THE ROCKAWAY HOTEL, BUILT IN 1870 ON THE EAST SIDE OF WHAT IS NOW AGAMONT PARK. THE ROCKAWAY WAS TORN DOWN IN 1916.

*Newport House and Shaw Path, Bar Harbor, Me.*

19. Today, a modern wharf in front of the Bar Harbor Inn sits close to the site of this steel pier built in the late 1880s. President William Howard Taft came ashore at the pier during his visit to the community. A private club on the grounds, The Reading Room, was a front to assist summer cottagers in avoiding Prohibition. The steel pier was torn down in 1930.

Steel Pier
Bar Harbor ME.

20. Balance Rock still remains along the Shore Path at the foot of Grant's Park, also known as Albert's Meadow. This erratic is granite, a type of rock different from the sedimentary strata it rests upon. Geologists believe that the huge boulder was left behind by a retreating glacier.

Balance Rock, Bar Harbor, Me.

Sorry not to see you Anna but went to Bar Har

21. HARDY'S POINT ALONG THE SHORE PATH IS LOCATED ON THE PROPERTY OF THE BAR HARBOR INN. ALSO CALLED THE TOW PATH IN EARLY MANUSCRIPTS AND ON POSTCARDS, THE SHORE PATH BEGINS AT THE TOWN PIER AND STRETCHES FOR THREE-QUARTERS OF A MILE TO WAYMAN LANE. MAINTAINED BY THE VILLAGE IMPROVEMENT SOCIETY, THE PATH IS OPEN TO THE PUBLIC THROUGH THE GRACIOUSNESS OF PRIVATE LANDOWNERS ALONG THE ROUTE.

Hardy's Point, Bar Harbor, Me.                                    214133

22. REEF POINT, ON THE SHORE PATH, WOULD LATER BE HOME TO RENOWNED LANDSCAPE ARCHITECT BEATRIX FARRAND. THOMAS MUSGRAVE'S ADJACENT ESTATE SPORTED A STONE AND WOOD TOWER. BUILT IN 1881, THE TOWER SHOWN HERE WAS EVENTUALLY TORN DOWN.

Bar Harbor, Me. Shore Path, Bar Island in Distance.

23. BUILT IN 1882, THE MALVERN HOTEL ON KEBO STREET, SOUTH OF MOUNT DESERT STREET, BOASTED NUMEROUS "COTTAGES" OF UP TO FOURTEEN ROOMS EACH. IT BURNED IN THE GREAT FIRE OF 1947. A SENIOR CITIZENS' HOUSING COMPLEX IS LOCATED THERE NOW.

Malvern Hotel
Bar Harbor M.E.

24. THE BELMONT HOTEL, BUILT IN 1879, WAS
LOCATED JUST EAST OF THE MALVERN HOTEL
ON MOUNT DESERT STREET. THE BELMONT WAS
DESTROYED IN THE GREAT FIRE OF 1947.

BAR HARBOR, ME. BELMONT HOTEL.

25. BUILT IN 1874 TO REPLACE A HOTEL THAT
BURNED DOWN THE PREVIOUS YEAR, THE ATLANTIC
HOTEL WAS LOCATED BETWEEN HANCOCK STREET
AND ATLANTIC AVENUE. A NEW OWNER CHANGED ITS
NAME TO THE LOUISBURG HOTEL IN 1887, NAMING
IT AFTER A SQUARE ON BEACON HILL IN BOSTON.
THE BUILDING WAS TORN DOWN IN 1939, ONCE IT
WAS NO LONGER ECONOMICALLY VIABLE.

6013. THE LOUISBURG, BAR HARBOR, MT. DESERT ISLAND, ME.

COPYRIGHT, 1901, BY DETROIT PHOTOGRAPHIC CO.

*Rec'd your letter will ans' soon*

*Thank you for the collar it is very pretty. Happy New*

*Year from Aunt Vilcar*

26. THE DE GREGOIRE HOTEL WAS NAMED AFTER THE WOMAN WHO ONCE HELD TITLE TO HALF OF MOUNT DESERT ISLAND—MARIE THERESE DE GREGOIRE, DAUGHTER OF FRENCH EXPLORER ANTOINE DE LAMOTHE CADILLAC. THE HOTEL, LOCATED ON THE NORTHEAST SIDE OF THE INTERSECTION OF EDEN AND WEST STREETS, OPENED IN 1907. IT WAS DESTROYED IN THE GREAT FIRE OF 1947. THE AREA IS TREES AND FIELD NOW.

Bar Harbor, Maine.  The De Gregoire.

27. LOCATED ON MAIN STREET, DIRECTLY
ACROSS FROM THE VILLAGE GREEN, THE HOTEL
FLORENCE WAS A RAMBLING WOODEN STRUCTURE
BUILT IN 1887. IT BURNED IN 1918 EXCEPT FOR
A PORTION OF THE BUILDING ON THE FAR LEFT.
RETAIL SHOPS LINE THE AREA NOW.

BAR HARBOR, ME.    HOTEL FLORENCE AND VILLAGE GREEN.

28. Mount Desert Island's original summer visitors were the Wabanaki people, who thronged to encampments along the shore. As increased economic pressure was brought on land values in the late 1800s, the local Native Americans found themselves pushed back to less and less desirable areas. This view was taken near the present site of the Bar Harbor Athletic Fields off Main Street after the Native Americans were uprooted from the shore near the Bar Island gravel bar.

Greetings
from
Bar Harbor.

THE INDIAN VILLAGE.

29. Lavish seasonal "cottages" sprang up on every shore and hilltop in Bar Harbor during the resort's Golden Age. Blair Eyrie was built in 1888 near present-day Highbrook Road. It was purchased by New York banker Dewitt Blair in 1901 but was demolished in 1935 as income taxes and the waning interest of the new generation of wealthy cottagers caused the area to lose favor. A nursing care facility occupies the site now.

Blaireyrie, Bar Harbor, Me. Residence of D. C. Blair.

30. Built in 1881 for J. Montgomery Sears of Boston, Briar Cliffe, also known simply as The Briars, was located along the Shore Path near the end of Wayman Lane. The house was eventually bought by Edward McLean, whose wife owned the Hope Diamond. Nelson Rockefeller was born in the house while it was being rented by his father, John D. Rockefeller, Jr. The main house was torn down in 1968.

BRIAR CLIFFE, BAR HARBOR, MAINE.
RESIDENCE OF EDWARD MC LEAN.

31. Home of James Blaine, U.S. senator, Speaker of the House, and two-time secretary of state, Stanwood was located along today's Highbrook and Norman Roads. Secretary of State Blaine lost his presidential bid in 1884 to Grover Cleveland. The house burned in the Great Fire of 1947.

*Stanwood, Home of late James G. Blaine, Bar Harbor, Me.* '09

32. One of the few remaining Golden Age mansions still open to the public, the Turrets on Eden Street is now a classroom and administration building at the College of the Atlantic. It was built in 1893 for J. J. Emery.

The Turrets, Bar Harbor, Me.

Handcolored

33. Although its formal name was Buonriposo, this Eden Street waterfront home was simply called the Fabbri Cottage by townspeople. It was built in 1904 for Ernesto Fabbri, whose brother Alessandro established a transatlantic radio station at Otter Cliffs. (A monument at a picnic area in Acadia National Park still notes that accomplishment.) The house was rebuilt after suffering major damage in a fire in 1918. It was torn down in 1963.

Fabbri Cottage, Eden Street, Bar Harbor, Me.

34. PUBLISHING MAGNATE JOSEPH PULITZER PURCHASED CHATWOLD, ON THE SHORE OFF SCHOONER HEAD ROAD, IN 1894. A FANATIC ABOUT QUIET, HE HAD THE IMPOSING GRANITE "TOWER OF SILENCE" BUILT TO KEEP OUT NOISE, INCLUDING THE FOGHORN ON EGG ROCK, DIRECTLY OFFSHORE IN FRENCHMAN BAY. THE HOUSE WAS DEMOLISHED IN 1945.

BAR HARBOR, ME. "CHATWOLD" HON. JOSEPH PULITZER'S HOUSE

35. SHOWPLACE GARDENS WENT HAND IN HAND WITH
ELABORATE "COTTAGES," AS SHOWN BY THIS ITALIAN
GARDEN AT KENARDEN, ON CROMWELL COVE. THE HOUSE
WAS BUILT FOR JOHN STEWART KENNEDY OF NEW YORK IN
1892. IT WAS TORN DOWN IN 1960, AND ANOTHER PRIVATE
RESIDENCE WAS ERECTED ON THE SPOT IN THE 1970S.

ITALIAN GARDEN, BAR HARBOR, MAINE

54176

36. The ornate garden at Beau Desert, an estate on the shore along Eden Street, looks to be the perfect place for children to play, providing they are on their best behavior. The house and grounds were built in 1882 for Walter Gurnee. The house was torn down in 1938, and the site later became an Oblate seminary. Vestiges of the gardens are still visible in the property's latest incarnation, College of the Atlantic.

Garden at Beau Desert, Bar Harbor, Me.

37. Kebo Valley Club, on the Eagle Lake Road, created its first six-hole course in 1892, making it the ninth-oldest golf course in the country. Over the years, several clubhouses have been built at various locations on the property. Although the tennis courts are long gone, the putting green remains near the latest clubhouse. Note the misspelling of the word Vallay; spelling errors were common on early postcards.

Kebo Valley Club
Bar Harbor Me.

38. PRESIDENT WILLIAM HOWARD TAFT (WITH BOW
TIE, IN THE CENTER) PLAYED KEBO VALLEY DURING HIS
VISIT IN JULY 1910. HE IS SHOWN ON THE SIXTEENTH
GREEN WITH THE BUILDING OF THE ARTS IN THE BACK-
GROUND. PRESIDENT TAFT SET A NEW "RECORD" RIGHT
AFTER THIS PHOTOGRAPH WAS TAKEN, SHOOTING A
27 ON THE PAR FOUR SEVENTEENTH HOLE.

Golfing at, Bar Harbor, Me.

214138

39. Built in 1903, the tony Bar Harbor Swim Club on West Street boasted a saltwater pool, where water was let in at high tide, then kept in so it could warm up. Tennis was also popular. The club was eventually replaced by the Bar Harbor Club. That building remains along West Street, just east of Bridge Street.

arrived Home
all right.
be glad.

Jeff—

Swimming Pool
Bar Harbor M.E.

40. BAR HARBOR'S ATHLETIC FIELDS WERE GIVEN TO
THE COMMUNITY BY THE OWNERS OF KENARDEN (SHOWN
IN CARD #35). THE VIEW WAS TAKEN FROM ALONG PARK
STREET NEAR THE SITE OF THE PRESENT-DAY MOUNT
DESERT ISLAND YMCA. THE HOUSE ON STRAWBERRY
HILL IN THE DISTANCE WAS LIKELY THE SPOT WHERE
THE VIEW OF THE TOWN ON CARD #1 WAS TAKEN.

Kennedy Field and Strawberry Hill

41. THE BAR HARBOR HORSE SHOW WAS THE PEAK EVENT OF THE SUMMER SEASON. IT WAS HELD OVER THREE DAYS EACH AUGUST IN MORRELL PARK, NAMED FOR COLONEL EDMUND MORRELL OF PHILADELPHIA. A VIEWING BOX WITH FEWER THAN A DOZEN CHAIRS COST THE PRINCELY SUM OF FIVE HUNDRED DOLLARS. THE GROUNDS AND RACETRACK WERE AT THE FOOT OF CHAMPLAIN MOUNTAIN WHERE THE RENOWNED JACKSON LABORATORY IS NOW LOCATED.

Bar Harbor Horse Show

42. DEVIL'S OVEN WAS WHAT NATIVE AMERICANS CALLED THE ROCK FORMATION CURRENTLY KNOWN AS THE OVENS. THEY BELIEVED IT WAS AN ENTRANCE TO HELL. LOCATED AT THE BASE OF CLIFFS BETWEEN HULLS AND SALISBURY COVES, THESE WAVE-SCULPTED CUTS AND EVEN A SMALL NATURAL BRIDGE WERE ONCE POPULAR DESTINATIONS FOR COTTAGERS' AFTERNOON JAUNTS. THE OVENS ARE ACCESSIBLE ONLY AT LOW TIDE AND ARE ON PRIVATE PROPERTY NOT OPEN TO THE PUBLIC.

216159

The Ovens, Mt. Desert Island, near Bar Harbor, Me.

43. VIEWS SUCH AS THIS ALONG OCEAN DRIVE IN
ACADIA NATIONAL PARK INSPIRED SUMMER VISITORS
TO FORM THE HANCOCK COUNTY TRUSTEES FOR PUBLIC
RESERVATIONS. THE GROUP BEGAN ACQUIRING LAND SO
THAT IT WOULD NOT BE USED FOR SEASONAL HOMES OR
FALL TO THE ISLAND'S BUSTLING LOGGING INDUSTRY.

The Ocean Drive and Otter Cliffs   Bar Harbor, Maine

44. Looking northeast along Ocean Drive toward Gorham Mountain (left) and the Beehive, the view today is little changed from that shown in a hand colored card published by Sherman's Book and Stationery Store in Bar harbor.

45. Sand Beach in Acadia National Park was privately owned until after the Great Fire of 1947. In 1911 the schooner "Tay," carrying a cargo of lumber and shingles, wrecked on the beach, with the loss of one life. The ribs of the schooner can still be seen when the dunes are eroded by fierce winter storms.

Sand Beach and Bee Hive Mountain, Bar Harbor, Me.

46. WHEN FIRST CREATED, THIS PORTION OF OCEAN DRIVE ON THE ACADIA NATIONAL PARK LOOP ROAD WAS OPEN TO TWO-WAY TRAFFIC. THE PARK, WHICH WAS THE VISION OF SUMMER RESIDENTS GEORGE B. DORR AND CHARLES ELIOT, CAME TO BE IN NO SMALL MEASURE THANKS TO THE FINANCIAL SUPPORT OF JOHN D. ROCKEFELLER, JR. HIS CREWS BUILT MANY SECTIONS OF MOTOR ROADS AS WELL AS THE CARRIAGE ROAD SYSTEM.

The Ocean Drive.

*Bar Harbor, Me.*

47. ACADIA NATIONAL PARK STARTED OUT IN 1916
AS SIEUR DE MONTS NATIONAL MONUMENT. IT BECAME
LAFAYETTE NATIONAL PARK IN 1919. THE NAME WAS
CHANGED TO ACADIA IN 1929. THE PARK HAS LONG BEEN
HOME TO ENDANGERED SPECIES SUCH AS THE BALD
EAGLES SHOWN HERE. ENDANGERED PEREGRINE FALCONS
ARE NOW NURTURED AND PROTECTED BY THE PARK.

AMERICAN EAGLES IN NEST, MT. DESERT ISLAND, ME.

48. Now called the Lower Mountain Road, this section of the Acadia National Park Loop Road between Cadillac Mountain and Jordan Pond was one of the first stretches; it was completed in 1924. Eagle Lake is to the right and Pemetic Mountain on the left. From the start, planners wanted the park to be accessible by automobile. Initially only a gravel way, the road was eventually paved and now stretches for a total of twenty-two miles.

The Mountain Road, Acadia National Park   Mt. Desert Island, Me.

49. THIS OLD FARMSTEAD NEAR GREAT HEAD AND SAND BEACH WAS ALREADY CRUMBLING WHEN THIS PHOTOGRAPH WAS TAKEN AROUND 1910. THE MOUNTAIN IN THE BACK IS THE BEEHIVE. IT SPORTED MORE TREE COVER THEN THAN TODAY DUE TO CHANGES CAUSED BY THE GREAT FIRE OF 1947. A LATER STRUCTURE NEAR THE SITE IS NOW USED BY THE PARK SERVICE TO HOUSE SEASONAL RANGERS.

Bee Hive Mt., Mt. Desert Island. On the "Ocean Drive" near Bar Harbor, Me.

50. The Beachcroft Trail on Huguenot Head, near Champlain Mountain, looks much the same today as it did nearly 100 years ago. The trail, which switchbacks up a steep mountainside, was named after the summer estate of the woman who donated money for its construction.

BEACHCROFT PATH, BAR HARBOR, MAINE.

82564

51. THE BUBBLES, SEEN FROM THE LAWN OF THE JORDAN
POND HOUSE, FORM ONE OF THE MOST DISTINCTIVE RIDGE-
LINES IN NEW ENGLAND. THE OLD FARMHOUSE BUILT ON
THE SITE IN 1896 BECAME FAMOUS FOR TEA AND POPOVERS.
ITS WALLS, LINED WITH BIRCH BARK, SOWED THE SEEDS OF
THE BUILDING'S DESTRUCTION WHEN IT BURNED IN 1979.
A NEW, LARGER FACILITY WITH RESTAURANT, TEA LAWN,
AND GIFT SHOP NOW OCCUPIES THE SITE.

Mt. Desert Island, Maine, The Bubbles.

52. Several trails up Dorr Mountain, formerly called Dry Mountain or Flying Squadron Mountain, can be accessed after crossing these stepping-stones at the outlet of the Tarn near Sieur de Monts Spring in Acadia National Park. Park cofounder George Dorr created a dam at the stepping-stones to help reshape a swampy area into a small reflecting lake.

STEPPING STONES ACROSS OUTLET TO SIEUR-DE-MONTS TARN, BAR HARBOR, MAINE.

82552

53. The attire was properly modest for these ladies enjoying a leisurely paddle on a pond near Bar Harbor. Canoeing, hiking in the hills and woods, and afternoon sails on the bay were the primary forms of recreation.

Courtesy of the Bar Harbor Historical Society.

6817. A LILY POND.                    BAR HARBOR, MAINE.

54. Going for "tramps"—long hikes with friends with an emphasis on good conversation—was a popular activity during Bar Harbor's heyday. Here a group pauses near the top of Huguenot Head on the Beachcroft Trail to admire the view to the south toward Otter Creek.

Courtesy of the Bar Harbor Historical Society.

OTTER CREEK GORGE FROM HUGUENOT HEAD, BAR HARBOR, ME.

55. Schooner Head, off Schooner Head Road, sported far fewer trees than today in this view showing the Brigham Cottage. The cottage burned in the Great Fire of 1947. The high headland to the right, at the tip of Schooner Head, is now occupied by a large private seasonal residence.

BAR HARBOR, ME.    SCHOONER HEAD.

56. LEGEND HOLDS THAT SO MUCH DYNAMITE WAS USED AT
ONCE ON THIS CUT ON THE CADILLAC MOUNTAIN SUMMIT
ROAD THAT THE BLAST CRACKED STONE FOUNDATIONS
MILES AWAY IN BAR HARBOR. BEFORE THE ROAD WAS
BUILT, VARIOUS METHODS HAD BEEN USED TO GET UP THE
MOUNTAIN—THE HIGHEST POINT WITHIN FIFTY MILES OF THE
EASTERN SEABOARD—INCLUDING A COG RAILWAY AND A
TOLL ROAD FOR HORSE-DRAWN CARRIAGES.

57. THE SUMMIT TAVERN WAS THE LAST OF A SERIES OF PRIVATELY OWNED OR OPERATED STRUCTURES TO GRACE THE TOP OF CADILLAC MOUNTAIN IN ACADIA NATIONAL PARK. OVER THE YEARS, BUILDINGS HAVE INCLUDED MULTISTORIED WOODEN HOTELS, BUT THE ONLY BUILDINGS NOW ARE A SMALLER COMBINATION GIFT SHOP AND REST ROOM AND A RADIO TRANSMITTER SHACK.

Visit Summit Tavern at Summit of Cadillac Mountain.
Here one can secure an Official Booklet of Acadia National Park.
Souvenirs, Photographs and Post Cards are on sale.
Sodas and Light Lunches served.

SUMMIT TAVERN, SUMMIT OF CADILLAC MOUNTAIN, ACADIA NATIONAL PARK, BAR HARBOR, ME.

842

58. Renting a rowboat on Eagle Lake was once all the rage. The device at left, set in a cove at the northwest corner of the lake, is part of a conveyor owned by a company that harvested ice from the lake until the 1950s. Part of the sluiceway remains on the lake bottom and can be seen when the light is right and the water low. The lake today is a public water supply; swimming and wading are not permitted.

Bar Harbor, Maine.  Eagle Lake from Currens Cove.

59. CANON BROOK, ON THE EAST SIDE OF CADILLAC MOUNTAIN, DROPS THROUGH AN INTERESTING GORGE, AND IN FACT USED TO BE CALLED CANYON BROOK. YEARS AGO SOME MAPMAKERS TOOK TO LABELING IT CAÑON, WITH THE SPANISH AFFECTATION. FOR SOME REASON, IN SUBSEQUENT VERSIONS THE TILDE OVER THE N WAS DROPPED. OTHERS COPIED THE MISTAKE. THE CURRENT NAME—CANON—GIVES NO HINT OF THE BROOK'S GEOGRAPHICAL SETTING.

BAR HARBOR, ME.   CAÑON BROOK FALLS.

60. FOR MANY PEOPLE, THE HUNDREDS OF STONE STEPS ON THE EMERY PATH ON FLYING SQUADRON MOUNTAIN (NOW DORR MOUNTAIN) IN ACADIA NATIONAL PARK ARE THE HALLMARK OF THE TRAIL-BUILDING GOLDEN AGE SPURRED BY THE VARIOUS VILLAGE IMPROVEMENT SOCIETIES. THE PARK'S COFOUNDER, GEORGE B. DORR, PERSONALLY SUPERVISED CONSTRUCTION OF THE EMERY PATH IN 1913.

LAFAYETTE NATIONAL PARK. STONE STAIRS ON EMERY PATH.

FLYING SQUADRON MOUNTAIN, BAR HARBOR, ME.

61. A bird's-eye view of Bar Harbor from Scott's Hill, site of the present-day Wonderview Inn.

*Birdseye View from Scotts Hill*
*Bar Harbor, ME.*

62. WITH BOTH SIDES OF THE STREET LINED BY DISTINCTIVE SHINGLE-STYLE DWELLINGS, IT IS NO MYSTERY HOW COTTAGE STREET, IN THE VILLAGE OF NORTHEAST HARBOR, GOT ITS NAME. IT IS NOW CALLED SOUTH SHORE DRIVE. THE HOUSES ON THE LEFT WERE PRIVATELY OWNED. THOSE ON THE RIGHT WERE PART OF THE KIMBALL HOUSE HOTEL COMPLEX. THE TOWER AND FLAG IN THE DISTANCE ON THE RIGHT SIDE OF THE STREET ARE AT THE ROCK END HOTEL. BOTH HOTELS ARE LONG GONE NOW.

*Just a reminder*
*Hope you have none like this. Lovingly*
*Cora.*

Cottage Street, Northeast Harbor, Me.

63. A brand-new Neighborhood House shines shortly after it was built in 1906 in Northeast Harbor. Now a popular community center and provider of children's programs, the Neighborhood House looks much the same today.

NORTHEAST HARBOR, ME.  NEIGHBORHOOD HOUSE.

64. THE ROCK END WAS ONE OF NORTHEAST HARBOR'S FINEST HOTELS WHEN IT WAS COMPLETED IN 1884. ORIGINALLY CALLED THE REVERE HOUSE, IT WAS LOCATED ON A LEDGE OVERLOOKING THE WATER AT THE END OF ROCK END ROAD. IT BURNED IN 1942.

Rock End House, No. East Harbor, Me.

65. THE KIMBALL HOUSE, BUILT IN 1886 AT THE CORNER OF KIMBALL ROAD AND SOUTH SHORE DRIVE, ACROSS FROM ST. MARY'S CHURCH, WAS DESIGNED BY JOHN CLARK OF BAR HARBOR. THE GRAND OLD HOTEL, BOASTING SEVENTY GUEST ROOMS, FADED FROM POPULARITY AND WAS TORN DOWN IN 1966.

NORTHEAST HARBOR, ME. KIMBALL HOUSE

66. JAMES TERRY GARDINER DESIGNED THE SPECTACULAR SARGEANT'S DRIVE, ALONG THE EAST SIDE OF SOMES SOUND, AT THE REQUEST OF SAMUEL DUNCAN SARGEANT. IN SEVERAL PLACES THE ROADWAY HAD TO BE LITERALLY BLASTED OUT OF SHEER GRANITE CLIFFS. PAVING AND SLIGHTLY WIDENING THE ROAD OVER THE YEARS OBSCURED THE EXACT ROCK FORMATION SHOWN IN THIS PHOTOGRAPH.

North East Harbor, Maine. Sargents Drive, looking up Somes Sound.

67. LOCAL HISTORIANS ARE NOT SURE OF THE PRECISE LOCATION OF THIS OLD MILL, WHICH WAS ALREADY FALLING DOWN WHEN THE PHOTOGRAPH WAS TAKEN AROUND 1905. MOUNT DESERT ISLAND WAS HOME TO DOZENS OF MILLS, WHICH PRODUCED LUMBER, WOOL, FLOUR, AND OTHER COMMODITIES. THE BEST EDUCATED GUESS IS THAT THE STRUCTURE WAS A SAWMILL BUILT BY ED SOMES ON THE STREAM BETWEEN LONG POND AND SOMES POND IN SOMESVILLE, NEAR ANOTHER ONE CALLED, APPROPRIATELY ENOUGH, ED'S POND.

Mt. Desert, Me.  The Old Mill.

68. ALONG WITH BEING ARGUABLY THE PRETTIEST VILLAGE IN MAINE, SOMESVILLE BEARS THE DISTINCTION OF BEING THE FIRST SETTLEMENT ON MOUNT DESERT ISLAND. IN 1761 ABRAHAM SOMES BUILT A LOG CABIN IN THE AREA WHERE THE VILLAGE NOW SITS. EXCEPT FOR PAVED ROADS INSTEAD OF DIRT, AND THE ADDITION OF A FEW MORE HOUSES, THE VILLAGE LOOKS MUCH THE SAME TODAY AS IT DID 100 YEARS AGO.

FROM THE COLLECTION OF BARBARA SAUNDERS.

848 Somesville, Me.
Main St.

69. WITH NARY A TREE IN SIGHT, THE LAYOUT OF THE VILLAGE OF SOMESVILLE IS EASY TO SEE IN THIS VIEW TAKEN FROM THE EAST SIDE OF THE HARBOR. THE STEEPLE BELONGS TO THE SOMESVILLE UNION MEETING HOUSE, WHICH WAS ERECTED IN 1852. THE CHURCH IS STILL ACTIVE TODAY.

849 Somesville, Me.

70. Considered the only true fjord on the East Coast, Somes Sound was carved by glaciers that covered the island with nearly a mile of ice. The ocean inlet, which is several hundred feet deep in places, nearly cuts Mount Desert Island in two. This view is taken from the north end of the sound looking south. Brown's Mountain, now called Norumbega, rises on the left; Robinson Mountain, now called Acadia, is on the right.

MT. DESERT ISLAND, ME. SOMES' SOUND.

71. Buildings cluster around the shore in Seal Harbor where only fields and parkland remain today. Seal Harbor was first settled in June 1809. It was formerly called Clement's Harbor. The large hotel at the upper right is the Sea Side Inn. The buildings with flags in the middle of the photograph are the Petit Hotel (left) and the Glencove (right).

B.D.T.

9-1-9

Seal Harbor, Me. from Ox Hill.

72. Begun in 1869 and expanded several times before 1895, the Sea Side Inn stood slightly up the hill overlooking the Seal Harbor Beach. It was acquired by the Rockefeller family and torn down in 1964. Its location is now a field.

Sea Side Inn, Seal Harbor, Me.

73. This stunning stone arch over a cleft known as Raven's Nest is the centerpiece of Sea Cliff Drive in Seal Harbor. The road, now owned by the town, was built in 1895 by George B. Cooksey, an English grain dealer from New York, to open up several hundred acres of property he purchased for development. The area is now an exclusive enclave of summer cottages owned by the rich and famous.

Seal Harbor, Maine. The Arch Bridge and Sea Cliff Drive.

74. THE SEAL HARBOR CONGREGATIONAL CHURCH, DESIGNED BY GROSVENOR ATTERBURY, WAS BUILT BY CHARLES CANDAGE IN 1902. IT REMAINED IN USE UNTIL IT WAS SOLD TO AN INDIVIDUAL IN 1989. THE CONGREGATION STILL MEETS IN THE ABBY CHAPEL IN SEAL HARBOR.

SEAL HARBOR, ME.   CONGREGATIONAL CHURCH.

75. THE EYRIE, THE SPECTACULAR SUMMER HOME OF ACADIA NATIONAL PARK'S MAIN BENEFACTOR, JOHN D. ROCKEFELLER, JR., STARTED OUT AS A MUCH MORE MODEST HOME. MR. ROCKEFELLER BOUGHT THE PROPERTY, OVERLOOKING LITTLE LONG POND IN SEAL HARBOR, IN 1910 AND IMMEDIATELY BEGAN EXPANDING THE HOUSE. FIFTY YEARS LATER, AFTER HIS DEATH, OTHER FAMILY MEMBERS OFFERED TO GIVE THE HOUSE TO ANY WORTHY ORGANIZATION OR EDUCATIONAL INSTITUTION, TO NO AVAIL. THE HOUSE WAS TORN DOWN IN 1963.

76. ARCHITECT DUNCAN CHANDLER DESIGNED
THIS PALATIAL SUMMER HOME ATOP OX HILL IN SEAL
HARBOR FOR EDSEL FORD. AFTER CHANGING HANDS
SEVERAL TIMES, SKYLANDS WAS MOST RECENTLY
PURCHASED BY LIFESTYLE MAVEN MARTHA STEWART.

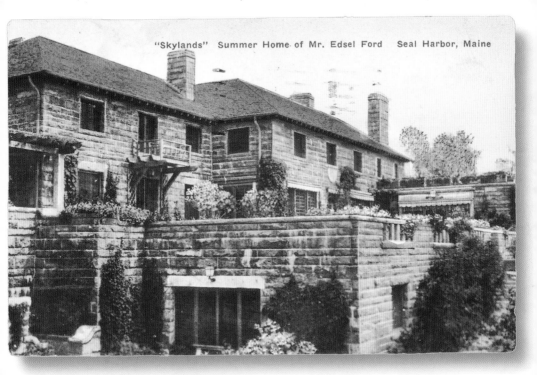

"Skylands" Summer Home of Mr. Edsel Ford   Seal Harbor, Maine

77. Little Long Pond in Seal Harbor was created by a natural seawall of cobblestones thrown up by winter surf. Owned by the Rockefeller family, the pond and the fields, forests, and carriage roads around it are open to the public. Mountains reflected in its waters include, from left to right, Jordan Mountain (now called Penobscot), the Bubbles (center), and Black Mountain (right), now called Pemetic.

Courtesy of the Bar Harbor Historical Society.

Long Pond, Mt. Desert Island, Maine.

78. Southwest Harbor's Main Street looks much different now than in this circa 1905 view looking north from approximately the corner of today's Wesley Avenue. Much of the downtown changed when a fire in 1922 destroyed five major buildings and damaged others. Southwest Harbor split from Tremont in 1905.

Main St., S. W. Harbor, Me.

79. THE SOUTHWEST HARBOR CONGREGATIONAL CHURCH, BUILT IN 1885 ON THE HIGH ROAD, IS STILL IN USE TODAY. ADDITIONS TO THE REAR OF THE STRUCTURE IN THE TWENTIETH CENTURY INCLUDED A PARISH HOUSE, OFFICES, AND SUNDAY SCHOOL ROOMS. THE CHURCH WAS THE FIRST ONE ORGANIZED ON MOUNT DESERT ISLAND, WITH THE CONGREGATION GATHERING IN OCTOBER 1792.

South West Harbor, Maine. Congregational Church.

80. The stately Claremont House Hotel continues to cater to summer visitors from its Clark Point site overlooking Somes Sound. Built in 1884, the building has expanded over the years, including the addition of a restaurant kitchen and dining room. Other houses on the grounds have been converted to guest space. The interior of the hotel underwent a major renovation in 1994.

Claremont House, S. W. Harbor, Me.

81. HIGH STREET, NOW HIGH ROAD, ATOP A HILL ON THE NORTH SIDE OF THE HARBOR IN SOUTHWEST HARBOR, PROVIDES EXCELLENT VIEWS TO THE EAST ACROSS SOMES SOUND TOWARD MANCHESTER POINT IN NORTHEAST HARBOR. THIS PORTION OF THE ROAD, AND THE STONE WALL, ARE NOW LOCATED ON PRIVATE WAYS NOT OPEN TO THE PUBLIC.

South West Harbor, Maine. View from foot of High Street, showing Somes Sound.

82. MARITIME COMMERCE HAS ALWAYS BEEN THE HALL-
MARK OF THE VILLAGE OF MANSET, WHICH IS PART OF
SOUTHWEST HARBOR. THIS AREA ON THE SOUTH SHORE
OF THE HARBOR TODAY HAS A HIGH CONCENTRATION
OF PIERS AND BOATING FACILITIES. THE HINCKLEY
COMPANY, A BOATBUILDING LEADER, IS CENTERED ON
THE SHORE OF THE COVE IN THE MIDDLE OF THIS VIEW.

Birdseye view of Manset, Me.

83. THE OCEAN HOUSE HOTEL, BUILT AROUND 1850, WAS A POPULAR SUMMER PLACE TO STAY IN MANSET, ON THE SOUTH SHORE OF SOUTHWEST HARBOR. THE HOTEL WAS TORN DOWN IN THE 1940S. IT WAS LOCATED AT THE TOP OF OCEAN HOUSE HILL ROAD NEAR THE PRESENT CATHOLIC CHURCH.

544 Southwest Harbor, Me. Ocean House.

84. MANSET HAS A DIRECT VIEW TO THE NORTH, FACING THE MOUTH OF SOMES SOUND. AT FERNALD POINT, ON THE LEFT OF THE SOUND IN THIS VIEW, THE FIRST ATTEMPT TO COLONIZE MOUNT DESERT ISLAND FAILED WHEN A BAND OF FRENCH JESUITS WHO CAMPED THERE IN JUNE 1613 WERE ATTACKED BY ENGLISH FORCES AND DRIVEN OFF. A MAJOR NATIVE AMERICAN VILLAGE, PRESIDED OVER BY CHIEF ASTICOU, WAS SITUATED DIRECTLY ACROSS THE SOUND TO THE EAST, ON MANCHESTER POINT IN NORTHEAST HARBOR.

Southwest Harbor, Me. Somes Sound.

*This space for address only*

85. THE BASS HARBOR HEAD LIGHTHOUSE, OVERLOOKING THE ENTRANCE TO THE HARBOR AND BLUE HILL BAY, IS A FAVORITE SCENIC SPOT EASILY ACCESSIBLE BY ROAD. THE LIGHTHOUSE WAS OPENED IN 1858; THE RED BEACON IN A BRICK TOWER WAS AUTOMATED IN THE LATTER HALF OF THE TWENTIETH CENTURY. THE GROUNDS ARE OPEN TO THE PUBLIC, ALTHOUGH THE KEEPER'S HOUSE IS A PRIVATE RESIDENCE.

Mt. Desert, Me. Bass Harbor Head Light.

86. TREMONT, ON MOUNT DESERT ISLAND'S WEST SIDE, SPLIT OFF FROM MOUNT DESERT IN 1848. WHEN ASKED WHAT TO NAME A NEW POST OFFICE FOR THE VILLAGE ON THE EAST SIDE OF BASS HARBOR, SOMEONE REMARKED TO A FEDERAL OFFICIAL, "NAME IT AFTER THE PRESIDENT [WILLIAM MCKINLEY] FOR ALL WE CARE." OFFICIALS DID, AND THE NAME MCKINLEY STUCK UNTIL THE MID-1960S, WHEN RESIDENTS PETITIONED CONGRESS TO CHANGE THE NAME OF THE TOWN TO BASS HARBOR. THIS VIEW IS FROM THE NORTH END OF THE HARBOR LOOKING SOUTH.

McKinley, Maine.  Looking down Bass Harbor.

87. THE VILLAGE OF BERNARD IS VIEWED ACROSS THE HARBOR FROM THE BASS HARBOR SIDE IN THE TOWN OF TREMONT. (THE LABEL AT LOWER LEFT REFERS TO BASS HARBOR'S ORIGINAL NAME OF MCKINLEY.) THE VANTAGE POINT IS NEAR THE SITE OF THE EXISTING MAINE STATE FERRY SERVICE TERMINAL, WHICH PROVIDES REGULAR SERVICE TO SWANS ISLAND AND FRENCHBORO.

McKinley, Maine.   Bernard from McKinley.

88. When Tremont was formed in 1848, some folks wanted to call it Mount Mansell, after the early English name for all of Mount Desert Island, but the name was rejected. Tremont eventually got its name from the three major peaks visible from the harbor, including, from the left, Bernard Peak and Mansell Peak on Western Mountain, and Beech Mountain, on the right. The first government meeting on Mount Desert Island, then a plantation, was held on Crocket Point in Tremont on March 30, 1776.

McKinley, Maine.  Bass Harbor Bay and Western Mt.

POST CARD

J.V.H. & CO.

For Correspondence

For address only

POSTAGE
DOMESTIC
1 CENT
FOREIGN
2 CENTS

89. The Great Fire of 1947 was a pivotal moment in Mount Desert Island's history. The fire began in a dump off the Crooked Road in Bar Harbor on October 17. Smoke billows high into the sky from the Crooked Road area in this view from the Bar Harbor Airport in Trenton, on the mainland. The mountains of Acadia National Park are in the background.

VIEW OF BAR HARBOR FIRE, OCT. 23, 1947

90. CREWS BATTLED THE GREAT FIRE FOR NEARLY A WEEK BUT LOST ABOUT 3,000 ACRES. THEN, ON OCTOBER 23, FLAMES WHIPPED BY GALE-FORCE WINDS BLACKENED ANOTHER 14,000 ACRES IN ONLY EIGHT HOURS. THE MALVERN HOTEL, WHICH IS SHOWN IN CARD #23, WAS DESTROYED BY THE FAST-MOVING FIRE.

VIEW OF BAR HARBOR FIRE, OCT. 23, 1947

MALVERN HOTEL AREA, BAR HARBOR, ME.

91. FIRE CREWS BACKED BY ARMY TROOPS COULD NOT SAVE MOST OF BAR HARBOR, EXCEPT FOR THE IMMEDIATE DOWN-TOWN. WITH FLAMES AND BURNING TREES BLOCKING ALL ROADS, SOME 400 PEOPLE WERE EVACUATED BY SEA FROM THE TOWN PIER. THE RUINS OF THE STATELY DeGREGOIRE HOTEL MARK THE EASTERN EDGE OF THE FIRE'S ADVANCE INTO THE BUSINESS DISTRICT. THAT HOTEL IS SHOWN IN CARD #26.

VIEW OF BAR HARBOR FIRE, OCT. 23, 1947

DEGREGOIRE HOTEL AREA, BAR HARBOR, ME.

92. Parts of utility poles rest in blackened trees near the Belmont Hotel after the 1947 fire hit Bar Harbor. (The Belmont is shown in card #24.) Three people died before the firestorm finally ran out of fuel in a rolling ball of flame that pitched over Great Head in Acadia National Park.

VIEW OF BAR HARBOR FIRE, OCT. 23, 1947

BELMONT HOTEL AREA, BAR HARBOR, ME.

93. Rubble was all that remained of this man's home near the Kebo Valley Club after flames swept across his neighborhood on the outskirts of town. In all, 17,188 acres—mostly in Bar Harbor and Acadia National Park—were blackened, 170 houses leveled, and 67 summer cottages destroyed in the Great fire of 1947.

VIEW OF BAR HARBOR FIRE, OCT. 23, 1947

FOREST STREET, BAR HARBOR, ME.

94. At the turn of the century, there were two options for traveling to Bar Harbor: train or steamship. The Bar Harbor Express made regular runs to Mount Desert Ferry—a wharf complex at Hancock Point, on the mainland—where passengers boarded steamships bound for harbors all around Frenchman Bay, including Bar Harbor. The last trains ran in the 1930s, and the tracks were long ago torn up.

M. C. R. R. The Bar Harbor Express.

95. CONSIDERED THE FINEST NAVAL COALING FACILITY IN THE WORLD WHEN IT WAS FINISHED IN 1903, THESE LONG DOCKS AND TOWERS WERE CAPABLE OF HOLDING 60,000 TONS OF COAL FOR THE GREAT WHITE FLEET. THE FACILITY WAS DEMOLISHED IN THE 1920S. THE SITE IS NOW LAMOINE STATE PARK, JUST NORTH OF MOUNT DESERT ISLAND.

UNITED STATES COALING STATION, BAR HARBOR, ME.  *Lamoine.*

96. Steamships serving all the towns on Mount Desert Island were the technological stars of their day. Built at Bath Iron Works in 1886, the "Sappho" was one of the most popular—and infamous. While people were boarding her in August 1889 at Mount Desert Ferry, the dock gave way, plunging scores of passengers into the water. Twenty people died.

"Sappho" at Bar Harbor, Maine.

97. BUILT AT BATH IRON WORKS IN 1902, THE SINGLE-SCREW-DRIVEN STEAMER "NORUMBEGA" WAS NAMED FOR THE MYTHOLOGICAL CITY OF GOLD SOUGHT BY EARLY EUROPEAN EXPLORERS. DESPITE RUNNING AGROUND AT CLARK POINT IN SOUTHWEST HARBOR IN 1912, SHE SAW YEARS OF DEDICATED SERVICE. SHE BURNED WHILE TIED TO A DOCK IN QUINCY, MASSACHUSETTS, IN 1934.

Bar Harbor, Me., Steamer Norumbega.

98. BOASTING DUAL PROPELLERS, THE STEAMSHIP "SIEUR DE MONTS" WAS BUILT BY NEAFIE AND LEVY AND PURCHASED BY THE MAINE CENTRAL RAILROAD IN 1905. THE SHIP CONTINUED SERVICE AROUND FRENCHMAN BAY UNTIL SHE WAS SOLD IN 1917.

Bar Harbor, Me., Steamer Steur De Monts.

99. STEAM WAS ALSO THE POWER OF CHOICE FOR THE SHORT-LIVED GREEN MOUNTAIN RAILWAY, A COG-DRIVEN LINE UP WHAT IS NOW CALLED CADILLAC MOUNTAIN. PASSENGERS TOOK A BUCKBOARD FROM BAR HARBOR TO THE NORTH END OF EAGLE LAKE, BOARDED THE STEAMER "WAUWIMET" FOR THE SHORT JAUNT DOWN THE LAKE TO THE RAIL TERMINAL, THEN SAT PATIENTLY WHILE THE WOOD-FIRED LOCOMOTIVE CHUGGED UP THE 1,532-FOOT PEAK. THE HIGH COST OF CORDWOOD FOR FUEL, AND COMPETITION FROM A CARRIAGE ROAD TO THE SUMMIT, BROUGHT ABOUT THE RAILWAY'S DEMISE IN 1893. COURTESY OF THE BAR HARBOR HISTORICAL SOCIETY.

100. ONE OF THE LAST STEAMSHIPS TO PROVIDE SERVICE TO BAR HARBOR, THE "MOOSEHEAD" PASSES BY THE BAR HARBOR BREAKWATER ON ITS WAY TO SEAL HARBOR, NORTHEAST HARBOR, SOUTHWEST HARBOR, AND TREMONT. BUILT IN 1911 AT BATH IRON WORKS, THE 185-FOOT VESSEL WAS WRECKED OFF THE COAST OF MASSACHUSETTS IN DECEMBER 1941. NEWPORT MOUNTAIN, LATER CHANGED TO CHAMPLAIN, IS IN THE BACKGROUND.

Steamer Moosehead passing The Breakwater,
Bar Harbor, Maine.

Newport Mt. 1090 feet high.

# To learn more THE FOLLOWING ORGANIZATIONS HOLD EXTENSIVE COLLECTIONS OF HISTORICAL PHOTOGRAPHS, BOOKS, ARTIFACTS, AND POSTCARDS FROM MOUNT DESERT ISLAND'S PAST.

## BAR HARBOR HISTORICAL SOCIETY MUSEUM
Ledgelawn Avenue
Bar Harbor, Maine 04609
207-288-0000

> Large collection of early photographs, artifacts, displays, and resources regarding local history. Original LIFE Magazine photographs and personal accounts of the 1947 fire.

## ABBE MUSEUM
PO Box 286
Mount Desert Street
Bar Harbor, Maine 04609
207-288-3519
abbe@midmaine.com

> Celebrating Maine's Native American heritage.

## GREAT HARBOR COLLECTION AT THE OLD FIREHOUSE
Main Street
Northeast Harbor, Maine 04662
207-276-5262

## HANCOCK HISTORICAL SOCIETY
Hancock, Maine 04640
207-422-3080

## ISLEFORD HISTORICAL SOCIETY
Isleford, Maine 04646
207-244-7853

**ISLESFORD HISTORICAL MUSEUM**
Islesford, Maine 04646
207-288-3338 (Acadia National Park)
Exhibits on early history of the region
known as Acadia. Artifacts, pictures,
household tools of Mount Desert.
Records of Cranberry Isles families.

**MDI HISTORICAL SOCIETY**
Route 198
Mount Desert, Maine 04660
207-276-9323
jroths@acadia.net
History of Mount Desert Island area,
including photograph and artifact
collections and library. Regular exhibits
and programs.

**NATURAL HISTORY MUSEUM,
COLLEGE OF THE ATLANTIC**
105 Eden Street
Bar Harbor, Maine 04609
207-288-5015
Exhibits depicting animal and plant
life indigenous to Mount Desert
Island and the Gulf of Maine.

**SEA SIDE HALL MUSEUM**
Atlantic, Swans Island, Maine 04685
207-526-4350
Local history with fisheries emphasis.

**TREMONT HISTORICAL SOCIETY**
Bass Harbor, Tremont, Maine 04612
207-244-3410

# About the Author

EARL BRECHLIN is a Registered Maine Guide and author of several books, including AN ADVENTURE GUIDE TO MAINE, HIKING ON MOUNT DESERT ISLAND, and PADDLING THE WATERS OF MOUNT DESERT ISLAND. He is editor of the MOUNT DESERT ISLANDER and former editor of the BAR HARBOR TIMES. An adjunct faculty member at College of the Atlantic in Bar Harbor, he was named Maine Journalist of the Year in 1997 and has served as president of the Maine Press Association and the New England Press Association.

**Acknowledgments** No book such as this could be produced without drawing on the knowledge of others. Particularly helpful in this endeavor was Deborah Dyer, inexhaustible curator of the Bar Harbor Historical Society. Also, "Framin'" Raymond Strout, a formidable historian in his own right; Jaylene Roths, curator of the Mount Desert Island Historical Society; Robert Pyle, librarian at the Northeast Harbor Library; Mary Jones of Southwest Harbor; Barbara Saunders; Lisa Plourde; Bonnie Lyons; Trina Travers, who put everything I do into correct English; Reverend Mac Bigelow; Reverend Richard Davis; and Connee Jellison of Bar Harbor. Special thanks to Harry Tracy of Tremont and the late James Strout of Bar Harbor, who were devoted local postcard collectors, as well as Karen Zimmermann of Z Studio design in Bar Harbor. Thanks also to all the people who have been kind enough over the years to sell or give me their old postcards. Last but not least, thanks to Karin Womer and all the good folks at Down East Books.